THE THEORY OF THE BUSINESS

HARVARD BUSINESS REVIEW
CLASSICS

THE THEORY OF THE BUSINESS

Peter F. Drucker

Harvard Business Review Press
Boston, Massachusetts

Copyright 2017 Harvard Business School Publishing Corporation
Originally published in *Harvard Business Review* in September–October 1994
Reprint #94506
All rights reserved

Printed in the United States of America

10 9 8 7 6 5 4 3 2 1

Cataloging-in-Publication data is forthcoming.

ISBN: 978-1-63369-252-7
eISBN: 978-1-63369-253-4

The paper used in this publication meets the requirements of the American National Standard for Permanence of Paper for Publications and Documents in Libraries and Archives Z39.48-1992.

THE HARVARD BUSINESS REVIEW CLASSICS SERIES

Since 1922, *Harvard Business Review* has been a leading source of breakthrough ideas in management practice—many of which still speak to and influence us today. The HBR Classics series now offers you the opportunity to make these seminal pieces a part of your permanent management library. Each volume contains a groundbreaking idea that has shaped best practices and inspired countless managers around the world—and will change how you think about the business world today.

THE THEORY OF THE
BUSINESS

Not in a very long time–not, perhaps, since the late 1940s or early 1950s–have there been as many new major management techniques as there are today: downsizing, outsourcing, total quality management, economic value analysis, benchmarking, reengineering. Each is a powerful tool. But, with the exceptions of outsourcing and reengineering, these tools are designed primarily to do differently what is already being done. They are "how to do" tools.

Yet "what to do" is increasingly becoming the central challenge facing managements, especially those of big companies that have enjoyed long-term success. The story is a familiar one: a company that was a superstar only yesterday finds itself stagnating and frustrated, in trouble and, often, in a seemingly unmanageable crisis. This phenomenon is by no means confined to the United States. It has become common in Japan and Germany, the Netherlands and France, Italy and Sweden. And it occurs just as often outside business—in labor unions, government agencies, hospitals, museums, and churches. In fact, it seems even less tractable in those areas.

The root cause of nearly every one of these crises is not that things are being done poorly. It is not even that the wrong things are being done. Indeed, in most cases, the *right* things are being done—but fruitlessly. What accounts for this apparent paradox? The assumptions on which the organization has been built and is being run no longer fit reality. These are the assumptions that shape any organization's behavior, dictate its decisions about what to do and what not to do, and define what the organization considers meaningful results. These assumptions are about markets. They are about identifying customers and competitors, their values and behavior. They are about technology and its dynamics, about a company's strengths and weaknesses. These assumptions are about what a company gets paid for. They are what I call a company's *theory of the business*.

Every organization, whether a business or not, has a theory of the business. Indeed, a valid theory that is clear, consistent, and focused is extraordinarily powerful. In 1809, for instance, German statesman and scholar Wilhelm von Humboldt founded the University of Berlin on a radically new theory of the university. And for more than 100 years, until the rise of Hitler, his theory defined the German university, especially in scholarship and scientific research. In 1870, Georg Siemens, the architect and first CEO of Deutsche Bank, the first universal bank, had an equally clear theory of the business: to use entrepreneurial finance to unify a still rural and splintered Germany through industrial development. Within 20 years of its founding, Deutsche Bank had become Europe's premier financial institution, which it has remained to this day in spite of two world wars, inflation, and Hitler. And, in the 1870s, Mitsubishi was founded on a clear and completely new theory of the business, which within 10 years made it the leader in an emerging Japan and within another 20 years made it one of the first truly multinational businesses.

Similarly, the theory of the business explains both the success of companies like General Motors and IBM, which have dominated the U.S. economy for the latter half of the twentieth century, and the challenges they have faced. In fact, what underlies the current malaise of so many large and successful organizations worldwide is that their theory of the business no longer works.

Whenever a big organization gets into trouble–and especially if it has been successful for many years–people blame sluggishness, complacency, arrogance, mammoth bureaucracies. A plausible explanation? Yes. But rarely the relevant or correct one. Consider the two most visible and widely reviled "arrogant bureaucracies" among large U.S. companies that have recently been in trouble.

Since the earliest days of the computer, it had been an article of faith at IBM that the computer would go the way of electricity. The future, IBM knew, and could prove with scientific rigor, lay with the central station, the ever-more-powerful mainframe into which a huge number of users could plug. Everything—economics, the logic of information, technology—led to that conclusion. But then, suddenly, when it seemed as if such a central-station, main frame-based information system was actually coming into existence, two young men came up with the first personal computer. Every computer maker knew that the PC was absurd. It did not have the memory, the database, the speed, or the computing ability necessary to succeed. Indeed, every computer maker knew that the PC had to fail—the conclusion reached by Xerox only a few years earlier, when its research team had actually built the first PC. But when that misbegotten monstrosity—first the Apple, then the Macintosh—came on the market, people not only loved it, they bought it.

Every big, successful company throughout history, when confronted with such a surprise, has refused to accept it. "It's a stupid fad and will be gone in three years," said the CEO of Zeiss upon seeing the new Kodak Brownie in 1888, when the German company was as dominant in the world photographic market as IBM would be in the computer market a century later. Most mainframe makers responded in the same way. The list was long: Control Data, Univac,

Burroughs, and NCR in the United States;
Siemens, Nixdorf, Machines Bull, and ICL in
Europe; Hitachi and Fujitsu in Japan. IBM,
the overlord of mainframes with as much in
sales as all the other computer makers put
together and with record profits, could have
reacted in the same way. In fact, it *should*
have. Instead, IBM immediately accepted the
PC as the new reality. Almost overnight, it
brushed aside all its proven and time-tested
policies, rules, and regulations and set up
not one but two competing teams to design
an even simpler PC. A couple of years later,
IBM had become the world's largest PC manufacturer and the industry standard setter.

There is absolutely no precedent for this
achievement in all of business history; it

hardly argues bureaucracy, sluggishness, or arrogance. Yet despite unprecedented flexibility, agility, and humility, IBM was floundering a few years later in both the mainframe and the PC business. It was suddenly unable to move, to take decisive action, to change.

The case of GM is equally perplexing. In the early 1980s—the very years in which GM's main business, passenger automobiles, seemed almost paralyzed—the company acquired two large businesses: Hughes Electronics and Ross Perot's Electronic Data Systems. Analysts generally considered both companies to be mature and chided GM for grossly overpaying for them. Yet, within a few short years, GM had more than tripled the revenues and profits of the allegedly mature EDS. And ten years later, in 1994, EDS had a market value six times the amount that GM had paid for it and ten times its original revenues and profits.

Similarly, GM bought Hughes Electronics —a huge but profitless company involved exclusively in defense—just before the defense industry collapsed. Under GM management, Hughes has actually increased its defense profits and has become the only big defense contractor to move successfully into large-scale nondefense work. Remarkably, the same bean counters who had been so ineffectual in the automobile business—30-year GM veterans who had never worked for any other company or, for that matter, outside of finance and accounting departments—were the ones who achieved those startling results. And in the two acquisitions, they simply applied policies, practices, and procedures that had already been used by GM.

This story is a familiar one at GM. Since the company's founding in a flurry of acquisitions 80 years ago, one of its core competencies has been to "overpay" for well-performing but mature businesses—as it did for Buick, AC Spark Plug, and Fisher Body in those early years—and then turn them into world-class champions. Very few companies have been able to match GM's performance in making successful acquisitions, and GM surely did not accomplish those feats by being bureaucratic, sluggish, or arrogant. Yet what worked so beautifully in those businesses that GM knew nothing about failed miserably in GM itself.

———————

What can explain the fact that at both IBM and GM the policies, practices, and behaviors that worked for decades—and in the case of GM are still working well when applied to something new and different—no longer work for the organization in which and for which they were developed? The realities that each organization actually faces have changed quite dramatically from those that each still assumes it lives with. Put another way, reality has changed, but the theory of the business has not changed with it.

Before its agile response to the new reality of the PC, IBM had once before turned its basic strategy around overnight. In 1950, Univac, then the world's leading computer company, showed the prototype of the first machine designed to be a multipurpose computer. All earlier designs had been for single-purpose machines. IBM's own two earlier computers, built in the late 1930s and 1946, respectively, performed astronomical calculations only. And the machine that IBM had on the drawing board in 1950, intended for the SAGE air defense system in the Canadian Arctic, had only one purpose: early identification of enemy aircraft. IBM immediately scrapped its strategy of developing advanced single-purpose machines; it put its best engineers to work on perfecting the Univac architecture and, from it, designing the first multipurpose computer able to be manufactured (rather than handcrafted) and serviced. Three years later, IBM had become the world's dominant computer maker and standard-bearer. IBM did not create the computer. But in 1950, its flexibility, speed, and humility created the computer *industry*.

However, the same assumptions that had helped IBM prevail in 1950 proved to be its undoing 30 years later. In the 1970s, IBM assumed that there was such a thing as a "computer," just as it had in the 1950s. But the emergence of the PC invalidated that assumption. Mainframe computers and PCs are, in fact, no more one entity than are generating stations and electric toasters. The latter, while different, are interdependent and complementary. In contrast, mainframe computers and PCs are primarily competitors. And, in their basic definition of *information*, they actually contradict each other: for the mainframe, information means memory; for the brainless PC, it means software. Building generating stations and making toasters must be run as separate businesses, but they can be owned by the same corporate entity, as General Electric did for decades. In contrast, mainframe computers and PCs probably cannot coexist in the same corporate entity.

IBM tried to combine the two. But because the PC was the fastest growing part of the business, IBM could not subordinate it to the mainframe business. As a result, the company could not optimize the mainframe business. And because the mainframe was still the cash cow, IBM could not optimize the PC business. In the end, the assumption that a computer is a computer—or, more prosaically, that the industry is hardware driven—paralyzed IBM.

GM had an even more powerful, and successful, theory of the business than IBM had, one that made GM the world's largest and most profitable manufacturing organization. The company did not have one setback in 70 years—a record unmatched in business history. GM's theory combined in one seamless web assumptions about markets and customers with assumptions about core competencies and organizational structure.

Since the early 1920s, GM assumed that the U.S. automobile market was homogeneous in its values and segmented by extremely stable income groups. The resale value of the "good" used car was the only independent variable under management's control. High trade-in values enabled customers to upgrade their new-car purchases to the next category—in other words, to cars with higher profit margins. According to this theory, frequent or radical changes in models could only depress trade-in values.

Internally, these market assumptions went hand in hand with assumptions about how production should be organized to yield the biggest market share and the highest profit. In GM's case, the answer was long runs of mass-produced cars with a minimum of changes each model year, resulting in the largest number of uniform yearly models on the market at the lowest fixed cost per car.

GM's management then translated these assumptions about market and production into a structure of semiautonomous divisions, each focusing on one income segment and each arranged so that its highest priced model overlapped with the next division's lowest priced model, thus almost forcing people to trade up, provided that used-car prices were high.

For 70 years, this theory worked like a charm. Even in the depths of the Depression,

GM never suffered a loss while steadily gaining market share. But in the late 1970s, its assumptions about the market and about production became invalid. The market was fragmenting into highly volatile "lifestyle" segments. Income became one factor among many in the buying decision, not the only one. At the same time, lean manufacturing created an economics of small scale. It made short runs and variations in models less costly and more profitable than long runs of uniform products.

GM knew all this but simply could not believe it. (GM's union still doesn't.) Instead, the company tried to patch things over. It maintained the existing divisions based on income segmentation, but each division now offered a "car for every purse."

It tried to compete with lean manufacturing's economics of small scale by automating the large-scale, long-run mass production (losing some $30 billion in the process). Contrary to popular belief, GM patched things over with prodigious energy, hard work, and lavish investments of time and money. But patching only confused the customer, the dealer, and the employees and management of GM itself. In the meantime, GM neglected its *real* growth market, where it had leadership and would have been almost unbeatable: light trucks and minivans.

A theory of the business has three parts. First, there are assumptions about the environment of the organization: society and its structure, the market, the customer, and technology.

Second, there are assumptions about the specific mission of the organization. Sears, Roebuck and Company, in the years during and following World War I, defined its mission as being the informed buyer for the American family. A decade later, Marks and Spencer in Great Britain defined its mission as being the change agent in British society by becoming the first classless retailer. AT&T, again in the years during and immediately after World War I, defined its role as ensuring that every U.S. family and business have access to a telephone. An organization's mission need not be so ambitious. GM envisioned a far more modest role—as the leader in "terrestrial motorized transportation equipment," in the words of Alfred P. Sloan, Jr.

Third, there are assumptions about the core competencies needed to accomplish the organization's mission. For example, West Point, founded in 1802, defined its core competence as the ability to turn out leaders who deserve trust. Marks and Spencer, around 1930, defined its core competence as the ability to identify, design, and develop the merchandise it sold, instead of as the ability to buy. AT&T, around 1920, defined its core competence as technical leadership that would enable the company to improve service continuously while steadily lowering rates.

The assumptions about environment define what an organization is paid for. The assumptions about mission define what an organization considers to be meaningful results; in other words, they point to how it envisions itself making a difference in the economy and in the society at large. Finally, the assumptions about core competencies define where an organization must excel in order to maintain leadership.

Of course, all this sounds deceptively simple. It usually takes years of hard work, thinking, and experimenting to reach a clear, consistent, and valid theory of the business. Yet to be successful, every organization must work one out.

What are the specifications of a valid theory of the business? There are four.

1. *The assumptions about environment, mission, and core competencies must fit reality.* When four penniless young men from Manchester, England, Simon Marks and his three brothers-in-law, decided in the early 1920s that a humdrum penny bazaar should become an agent of social change, World War I had profoundly shaken their country's class structure. It had also created masses of new buyers for good-quality, stylish, but cheap merchandise like lingerie, blouses, and stockings—Marks and

Spencer's first successful product categories. Marks and Spencer then systematically set to work developing brand-new and unheard-of core competencies. Until then, the core competence of a merchant was the ability to buy well. Marks and Spencer decided that it was the merchant, rather than the manufacturer, who knew the customer. Therefore, the merchant, not the manufacturer, should design the products, develop them, and find producers to make the goods to his design, specifications, and costs. This new definition of the merchant took five to eight years to develop and make acceptable to traditional suppliers, who had always seen themselves as "manufacturers," not "subcontractors."

2. *The assumptions in all three areas have to fit one another.* This was perhaps GM's greatest strength in the long decades of its ascendancy. Its assumptions about the market and about the optimum manufacturing process were a perfect fit. GM decided in the mid-1920s that it also required new and as-yet-unheard-of core competencies: financial control of the manufacturing process and a theory of capital allocations. As a result, GM invented modern cost accounting and

the first rational capital-allocation process.

3. *The theory of the business must be known and understood throughout the organization.* That is easy in an organization's early days. But as it becomes successful, an organization tends increasingly to take its theory for granted, becoming less and less conscious of it. Then the organization becomes sloppy. It begins to cut corners. It begins to pursue what is expedient rather than what is right. It stops thinking. It stops questioning. It remembers the answers but has forgotten the questions. The theory of

the business becomes "culture." But culture is no substitute for discipline, and the theory of the business is a discipline.

4. *The theory of the business has to be tested constantly.* It is not graven on tablets of stone. It is a hypothesis. And it is a hypothesis about things that are in constant flux—society, markets, customers, technology. And so, built into the theory of the business must be the ability to change itself.

Some theories of the business are so powerful that they last for a long time. But being human artifacts, they don't last forever, and, indeed, today they rarely last for very long at all. Eventually every theory of the business becomes obsolete and then invalid. That is precisely what happened to those on which the great U.S. businesses of the 1920s were built. It happened to the GMs and the AT&Ts. It has happened to IBM. It is clearly happening today to Deutsche Bank and its theory of the universal bank. It is also clearly happening to the rapidly unraveling Japanese *keiretsu*.

The first reaction of an organization whose theory is becoming obsolete is almost always a defensive one. The tendency is to put one's head in the sand and pretend that nothing is happening. The next reaction is an attempt to patch, as GM did in the early 1980s or as Deutsche Bank is doing today. Indeed, the sudden and completely unexpected crisis of one big German company after another for which Deutsche Bank is the "house bank" indicates that its theory no longer works. That is, Deutsche Bank no longer does what it was designed to do: provide effective governance of the modern corporation.

But patching never works. Instead, when a theory shows the first signs of becoming obsolete, it is time to start thinking again, to ask again which assumptions about the environment, mission, and core competencies reflect reality most accurately—with the clear premise that our historically transmitted assumptions, those with which all of us grew up, no longer suffice.

***

What, then, needs to be done? There is a need for preventive care—that is, for building into the organization systematic monitoring and testing of its theory of the business. There is a need for early diagnosis. Finally, there is a need to rethink a theory that is stagnating and to take effective action in order to change policies and practices, bringing the organization's behavior in line with the new realities of its environment, with a new definition of its mission, and with new core competencies to be developed and acquired.

PREVENTIVE CARE

There are only two preventive measures. But, if used consistently, they should keep an organization alert and capable of rapidly changing itself and its theory. The first measure is what I call *abandonment*. Every three years, an organization should challenge every product, every service, every policy, every distribution channel with the question, If we were not in it already, would we be going into it now? By questioning accepted policies and routines, the organization forces itself to think about its theory. It forces itself to test assumptions. It forces itself to ask: Why didn't this work, even though it looked so promising when we went into it five years ago? Is it because we made a mistake? Is it because we did the wrong things? Or is it because the right things didn't work?

Without systematic and purposeful abandonment, an organization will be overtaken by events. It will squander its best resources on things it should never have been doing or should no longer do. As a result, it will lack the resources, especially capable people, needed to exploit the opportunities that arise when markets, technologies, and core competencies change. In other words, it will be unable to respond constructively to the opportunities that are created when its theory of the business becomes obsolete.

The second preventive measure is to study what goes on outside the business, and especially to study *noncustomers*. Walk-around management became fashionable a few years back. It is important. And so is knowing as much as possible about one's customers—the area, perhaps, where information technology is making the most rapid advances. But the first signs of fundamental change rarely appear within one's own organization or among one's own customers. Almost always they show up first among one's noncustomers. Noncustomers always outnumber customers. Wal-Mart, today's retail giant, has 14% of the U.S. consumer-goods market. That means 86% of the market is noncustomers.

In fact, the best recent example of the importance of the noncustomer is U.S. department stores. At their peak some 20 years ago, department stores served 30% of the U.S. nonfood retail market. They questioned their customers constantly, studied them, surveyed them. But they paid no attention to the 70% of the market who were not their customers. They saw no reason why they should. Their theory of the business assumed that most people who could afford to shop in department stores did. Fifty years ago, that assumption fit reality. But when the baby boomers came of age, it ceased to be valid. For the dominant group among baby boomers—women in educated two-income families—it was not money that determined where to shop. Time was the primary factor, and this generation's women could not afford to spend their time shopping in department stores. Because department stores looked only at their own customers, they did not recognize this change until a few years ago. By then, business was already drying up. And it was too late to get the baby boomers back. The department stores learned the hard way that although being customer driven is vital, it is not enough. An organization must be market driven too.

EARLY DIAGNOSIS

To diagnose problems early, managers must pay attention to the warning signs. A theory of the business always becomes obsolete when an organization attains its original objectives. Attaining one's objectives, then, is not cause for celebration; it is cause for new thinking.

AT&T accomplished its mission to give every U.S. family and business access to the telephone by the mid-1950s. Some executives then said it was time to reassess the theory of the business and, for instance, separate local service—where the objectives had been reached—from growing and future businesses, beginning with long-distance service and extending into global telecommunications. Their arguments went unheeded, and a few years later AT&T began to flounder, only to be rescued by antitrust, which did by fiat what the company's management had refused to do voluntarily.

Rapid growth is another sure sign of crisis in an organization's theory. Any organization that doubles or triples in size within a fairly short period of time has necessarily outgrown its theory. Even Silicon Valley has learned that beer bashes are no longer adequate for communication once a company has grown so big that people have to wear name tags. But such growth challenges much deeper assumptions, policies, and habits. To continue in health, let alone grow, the organization has to ask itself again the questions about its environment, mission, and core competencies.

There are two more clear signals that an organization's theory of the business is no longer valid. One is unexpected success—whether one's own or a competitor's. The other is unexpected failure—again, whether one's own or a competitor's.

At the same time that Japanese automobile imports had Detroit's Big Three on the ropes, Chrysler registered a totally unexpected success. Its traditional passenger cars were losing market share even faster than GM's and Ford's were. But sales of its Jeep and its new minivans—an almost accidental development—skyrocketed. At the time, GM was the leader of the U.S. light-truck market and unchallenged in the design and quality of its products, but it wasn't paying any attention to its light-truck capacity. After all, minivans and light trucks had always been classified as commercial rather than passenger vehicles in traditional statistics, even though most of them are now being bought as passenger vehicles. However, had it paid attention to the success of its weaker competitor, Chrysler, GM might have realized much earlier that its assumptions about both its market and its core competencies were no longer valid. From the beginning, the minivan and light-truck market was not an income-class market and was little influenced by trade-in prices. And, paradoxically, light trucks were the one area in which GM, 15 years ago, had already moved quite far toward what we now call lean manufacturing.

Unexpected failure is as much a warning as unexpected success and should be taken as seriously as a 60-year-old man's first "minor" heart attack. Sixty years ago, in the midst of the Depression, Sears decided that automobile insurance had become an "accessory" rather than a financial product and that selling it would therefore fit its mission as being the informed buyer for the American family. Everyone thought Sears was crazy. But automobile insurance became Sears's most profitable business almost instantly. Twenty years later, in the 1950s, Sears decided that diamond rings had become a necessity rather than a luxury, and the company became the world's largest—and probably most profitable—diamond retailer. It was only logical for Sears to decide in 1981 that investment products had become consumer goods for the American family. It bought Dean Witter and moved its offices into Sears stores. The move was a total disaster. The U.S. public clearly did not consider its financial needs to be "consumer products." When Sears finally gave up and decided to run Dean Witter as a separate business outside Sears stores, Dean Witter at once began to blossom. In 1992, Sears sold it at a tidy profit.

Had Sears seen its failure to become the American family's supplier of investments as a failure of its theory and not as an isolated incident, it might have begun to restructure and reposition itself ten years earlier than it actually did, when it still had substantial market leadership. For Sears might then have seen, as several of its competitors like J.C. Penney immediately did, that the Dean Witter failure threw into doubt the entire concept of market homogeneity—the very concept on which Sears and other mass retailers had based their strategy for years.

CURE

Traditionally, we have searched for the miracle worker with a magic wand to turn an ailing organization around. To establish, maintain, and restore a theory, however, does not require a Genghis Khan or a Leonardo da Vinci in the executive suite. It is not genius; it is hard work. It is not being clever; it is being conscientious. It is what CEOs are paid for.

There are indeed quite a few CEOs who have successfully changed their theory of the business. The CEO who built Merck into the world's most successful pharmaceutical business by focusing solely on the research and development of patented, high-margin breakthrough drugs radically changed the company's theory by acquiring a large distributor of generic and nonprescription drugs. He did so without a "crisis," while Merck was ostensibly doing very well. Similarly, a few years ago, the new CEO of Sony, the world's best-known manufacturer of consumer electronic hardware, changed the company's theory of the business. He acquired a Hollywood movie production company and, with that acquisition, shifted the organization's center of gravity from being a hardware manufacturer in search of software to being a software producer that creates a market demand for hardware.

But for every one of these apparent miracle workers, there are scores of equally capable CEOs whose organizations stumble. We can't rely on miracle workers to rejuvenate an obsolete theory of the business any more than we can rely on them to cure other types of serious illness. And when one talks to these supposed miracle workers, they deny vehemently that they act by charisma, vision, or, for that matter, the laying on of hands. They start out with diagnosis and analysis. They accept that attaining objectives and rapid growth demand a serious rethinking of the theory of the business. They do not dismiss unexpected failure as the result of a subordinate's incompetence or as an accident but treat it as a symptom of "systems failure." They do not take credit for unexpected success but treat it as a challenge to their assumptions.

They accept that a theory's obsolescence is a degenerative and, indeed, life-threatening disease. And they know and accept the surgeon's time-tested principle, the oldest principle of effective decision making: A degenerative disease will not be cured by procrastination. It requires decisive action.

ABOUT THE AUTHOR

Peter F. Drucker was a writer, consultant, and professor of social science and management at Claremont Graduate University in California. His thirty-nine books have been published in more than seventy languages. He founded the Peter F. Drucker Foundation for Nonprofit Management, and counseled thirteen governments, public services institutions, and major corporations.

Article Summary

Idea in Brief

In his thirty-first article for HBR, Peter F. Drucker argues that what underlies the current malaise of so many large and successful organizations world-wide is that their theory of the business no longer works. The story is a familiar one: a company that was a superstar only yesterday finds itself stag-nating and frustrated, in trouble and, often, in a seemingly unmanageable crisis. The root cause of nearly every one of these crises is not that things are being done poorly. It is not even that the wrong things are being done. Indeed, in most cases, the right things are being done—but fruitlessly.

What accounts for this apparent paradox? The assumptions on which the organization has been built and is being run no longer fit reality. These are the assumptions that shape any organization's behavior, dictate its decisions about what to do and what not to do, and define what an organization considers meaningful results. These assumptions are what Drucker calls a company's theory of the business.

Every organization, whether a business or not, has a theory of the business. The theory of the business explains both the successes of companies like General Motors and IBM, which have dominated the U.S. economy for the latter half of the twentieth century, and the challenges they have faced.

Some theories of the business are so powerful that they last for a long time. But being human artifacts, they don't last forever, and today they rarely last for very long at all. Eventually, every theory of the business becomes obsolete and then invalid. When a theory shows the first signs of becoming obsolete, it is time to start rethinking the theory, with the clear premise that our historically transmitted assumptions no longer suffice.

The most important management ideas all in one place.

We hope you enjoyed this book from *Harvard Business Review*. For the best ideas HBR has to offer turn to HBR's 10 Must Reads Boxed Set. From books on leadership and strategy to managing yourself and others, this 6-book collection delivers articles on the most essential business topics to help you succeed.

HBR's 10 Must Reads Series

The definitive collection of ideas and best practices on our most sought-after topics from the best minds in business.

- Change Management
- Collaboration
- Communication
- Emotional Intelligence
- Innovation
- Leadership
- Making Smart Decisions

- Managing Across Cultures
- Managing People
- Managing Yourself
- Strategic Marketing
- Strategy
- Teams
- The Essentials

hbr.org/mustreads

Buy for your team, clients, or event.
Visit hbr.org/bulksales for quantity discount rates.